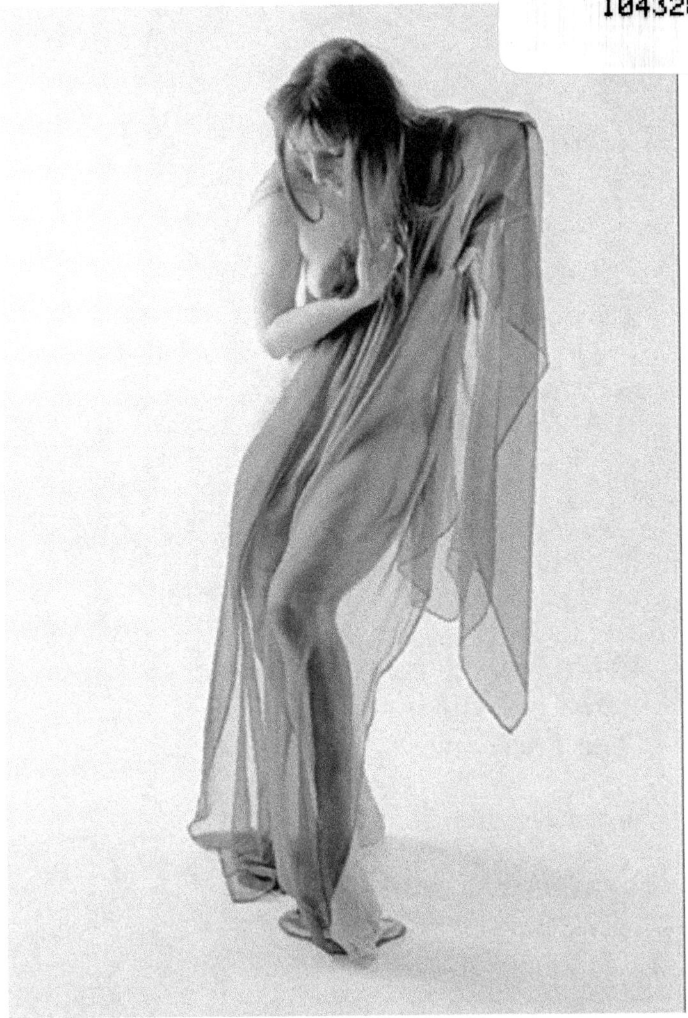

A Woman's Journey

Artistic Nude Poetry

Bev Pogreba & Fritz Penning

i find myself

With more refinement
   I'll go back
Back to the spontaneity
   And energy I had

With more dedication
   And appreciation
Of what I had
   I'll go back

With the same loving audience
   And the same sweet affairs
I'll go back

I have the want
   The need and
Certainly the greed

But it's all I have left
   That and the time to dream
Of what I had.

TITLES

Little Girls
growing up
in love

One day soon
the dangers
induce a change

Friends change
Lovers change
Sometimes
Hollywood Gold
with a Latin flair
equal reality

I find myself
trembling
of sweet caring
while kisses end

From California
to Colorado
always wishing
I was there.

Preface and Acknowledgements

The poems reveal a thread of commonality – the emotional highs and lows of falling in and out of love, the need and longing to grow up fast, the revelation of mistakes made and the knowledge that is gained in the end.

I hope these poems speak to others who have loved and lost and understand it is a journey that is bittersweet and necessary to live a full life.

Thank you to the beautiful women who inspired the idea of combining photographic images and poetry. The photographs are presented as art capturing the beauty of the female body.

A friend said it well after I expressed some concern with displaying the photos publicly: "I think the body needs to be recorded."

Bev Pogreba

The call to photograph the performing arts is irresistible. It is a privilege to capture and record talent that has taken many years to perfect. Combining this new technology of digital composition and presentation achieves results not available in years past.

Many years of photographing the elegance of dancers and performing artists as they portray themselves or role-play has created a library of images that begs to be shared.

The models present themselves naturally and are captured as they perform. Most noteworthy, while being photographed, they are not influenced by external sources. I am thankful for their trust.

Fritz Penning

Our heartfelt thanks to the many who have given so much to make this book possible.

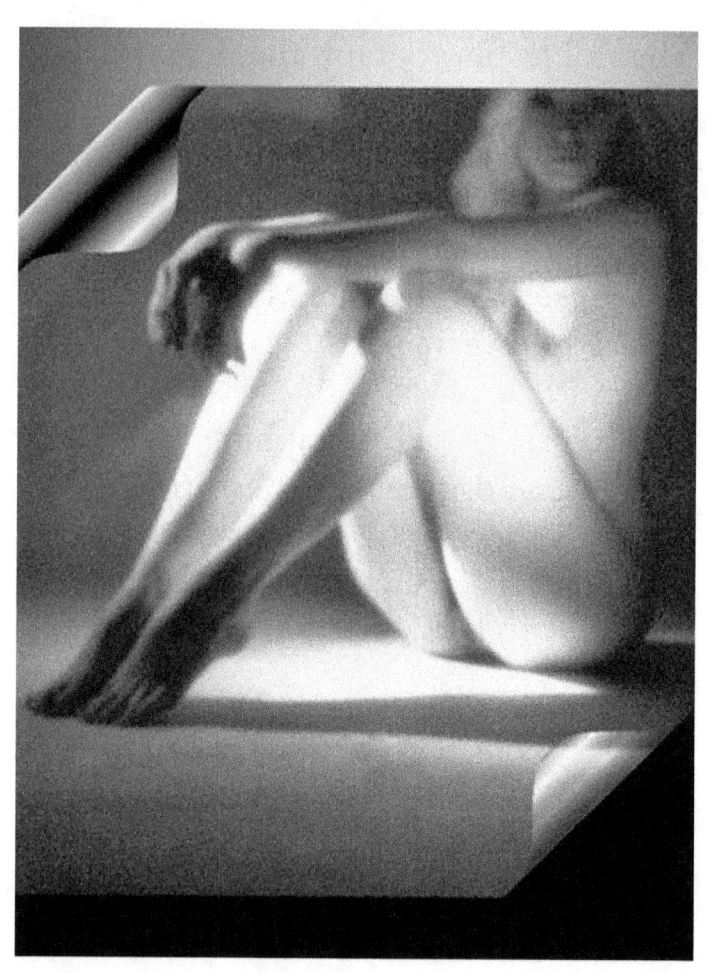

Little Girls

Little Girls

trying hard

to grow up fast

But after reaching motherhood

start longing

for the past

Their eyes have been overcome

by lovers who would seize them

They waited too long

for the right man

to please them.

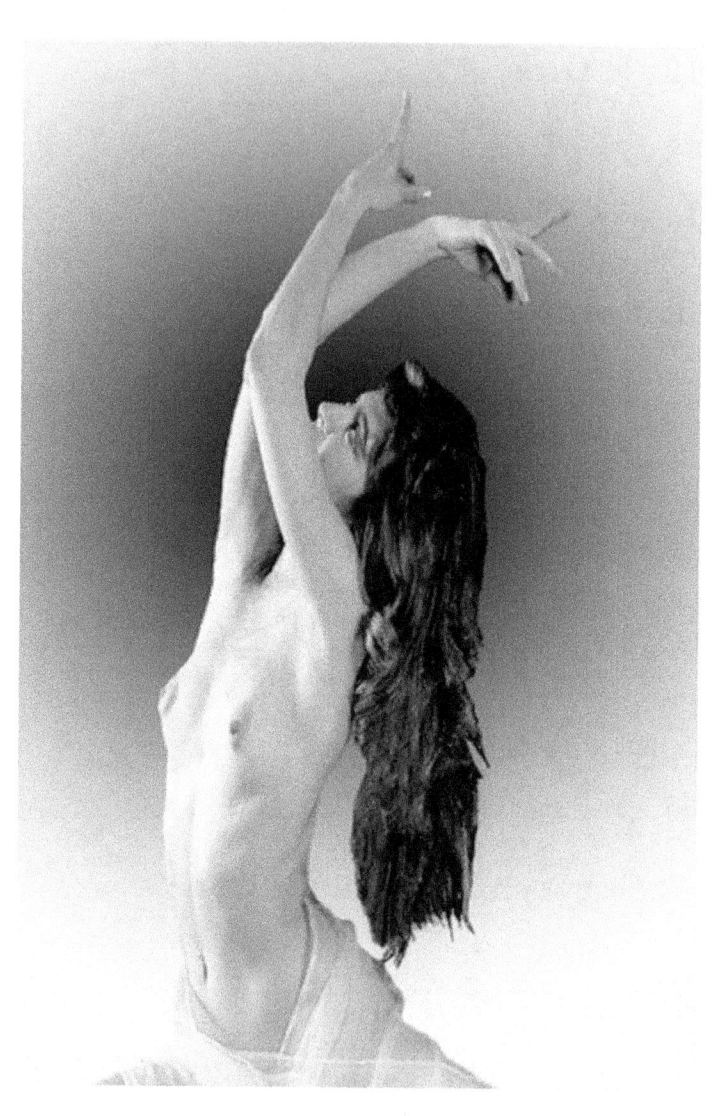

Growing Up

It is my splendor

to have

then surrender

the imperfections

I dare to own

I'd love to use them

abuse them

caress and then

mold them

to perfection.

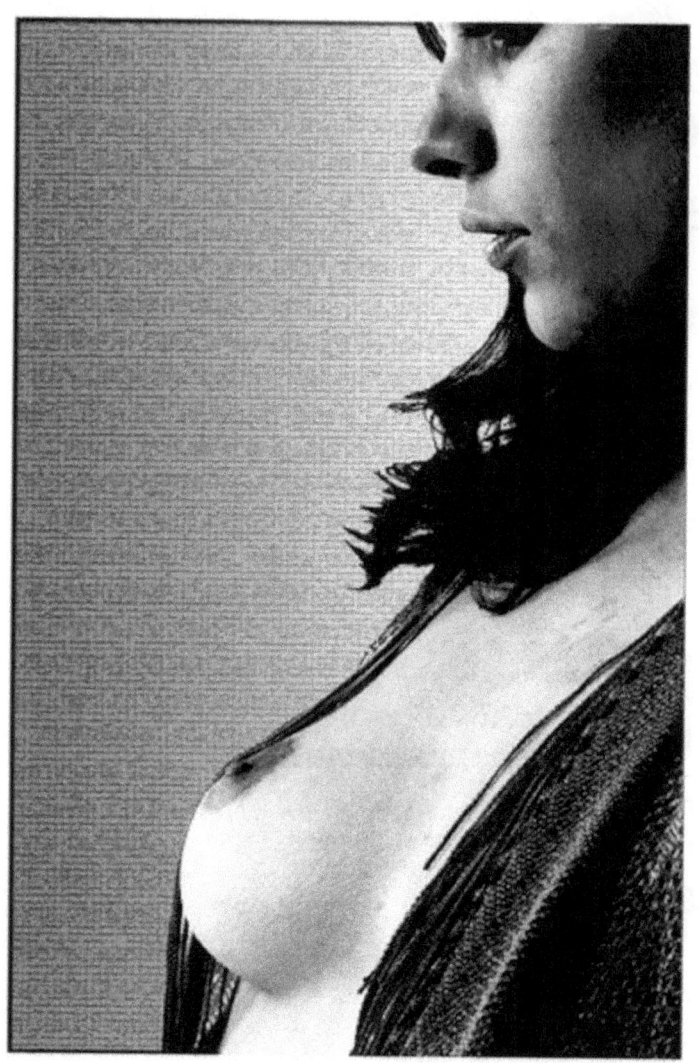

in love

You are

the wings of my dreams

the pulse of my spirit

the root of my soul

The restless sea and the endless sky

resembles the crystal clear love

I will always express

For you

I will become my own self worth

Because of you

I have a reason to live.

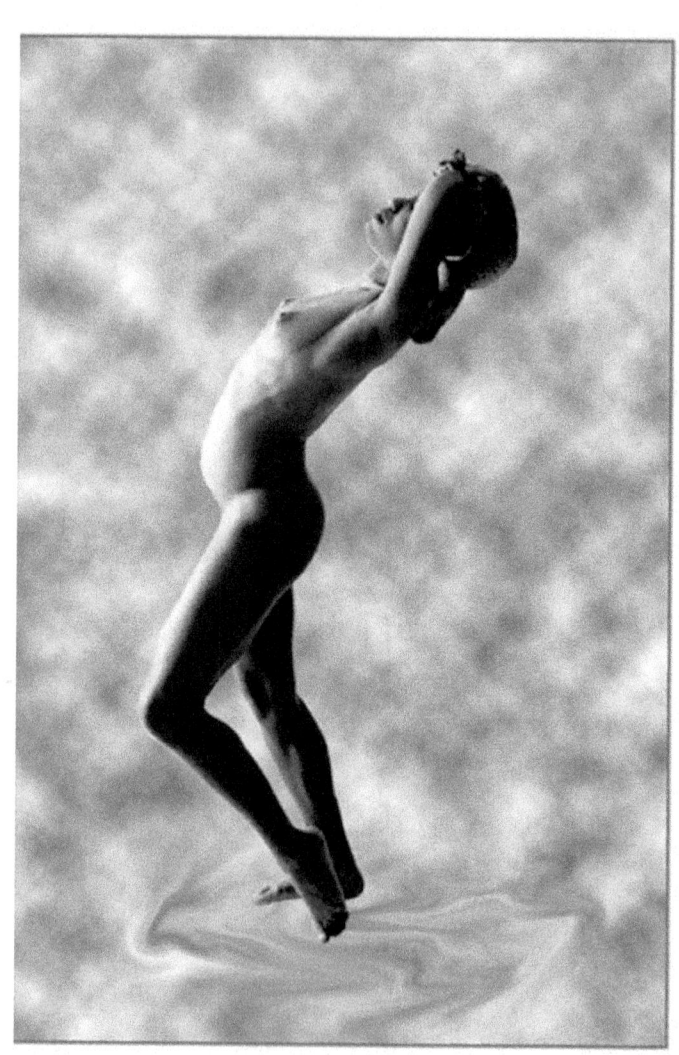

One day soon

With a love

I could have won

came a love

I should have lost

The pleasure of caring

loses its meaning

when the one you care for decides

not to care

How can you have such a big heart

and break one as big as mine?

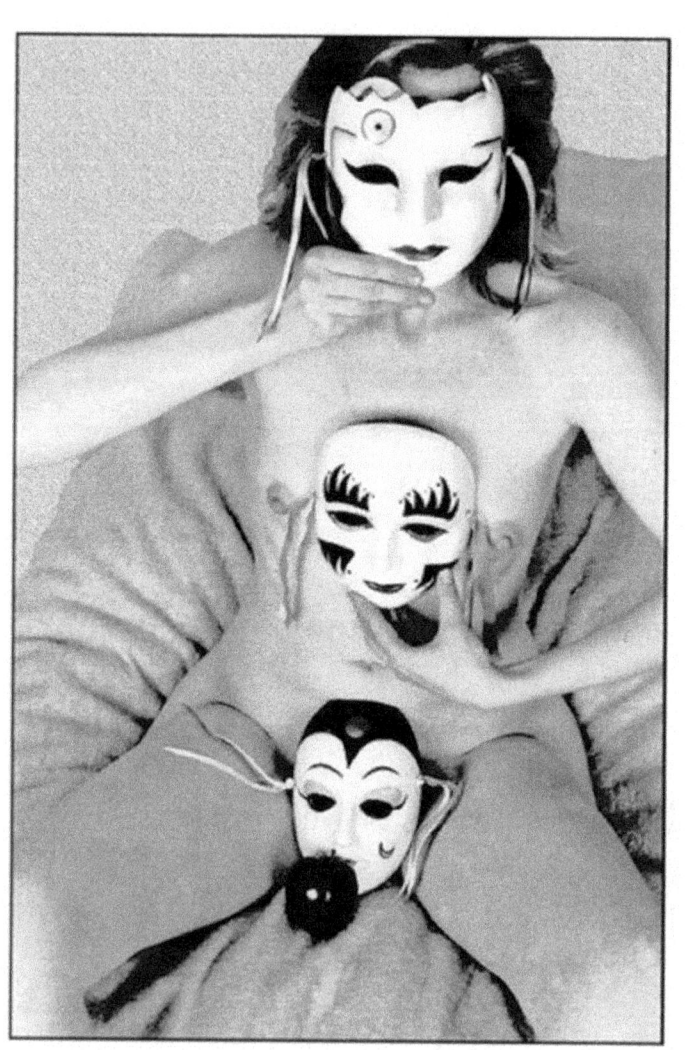

the dangers

Never will I be

changed into

another's image

A fever

is beginning

to emerge

Now all I need

is time

energy

and space to Breathe !

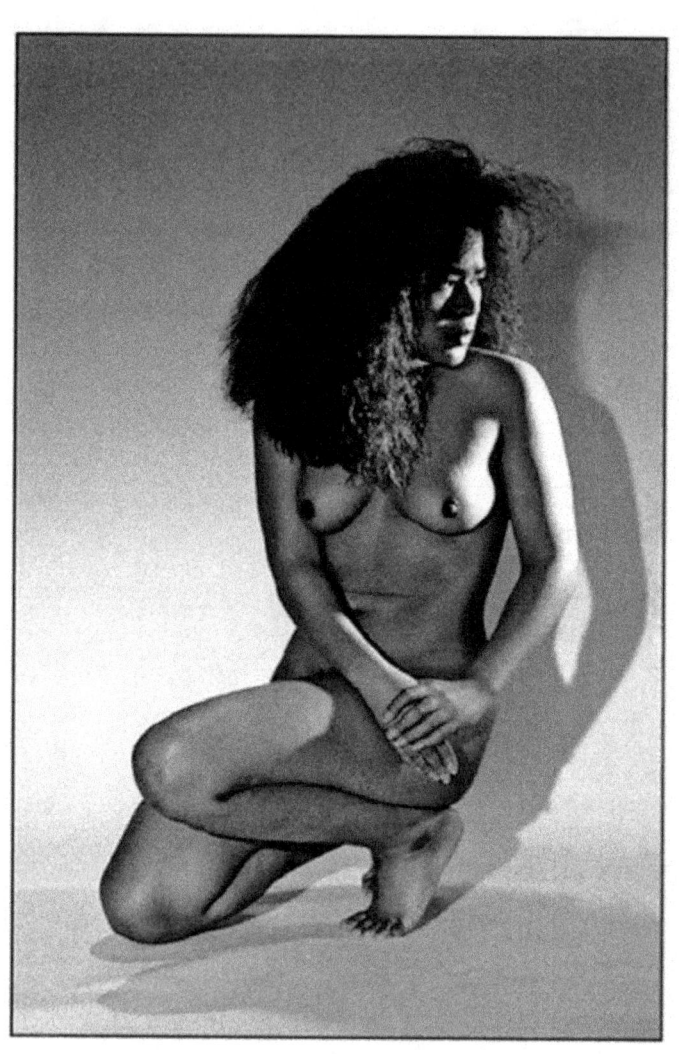

induce a change

Night time

so precious and dear

My mind becomes clear

as I gather a tear

Wishing you were here

to comfort my fear

And share one more year

of night times.

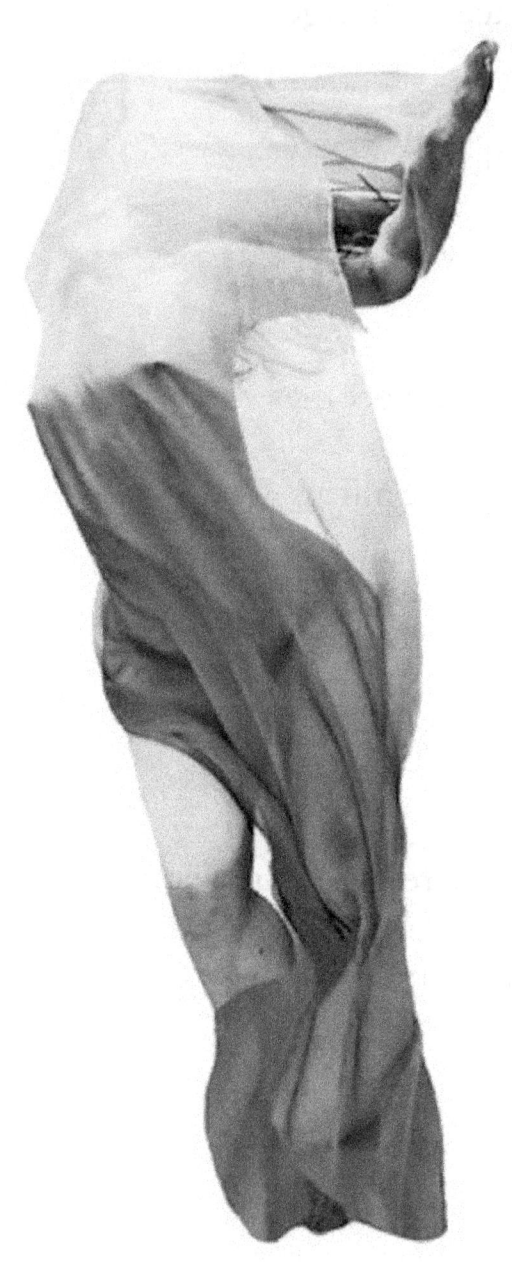

Friends change

Cocktails and busy tails

too busy to live

I have forty dreams

but know my limits

I limit the cocktails

and the busy tails

And limit my

circle of friends.

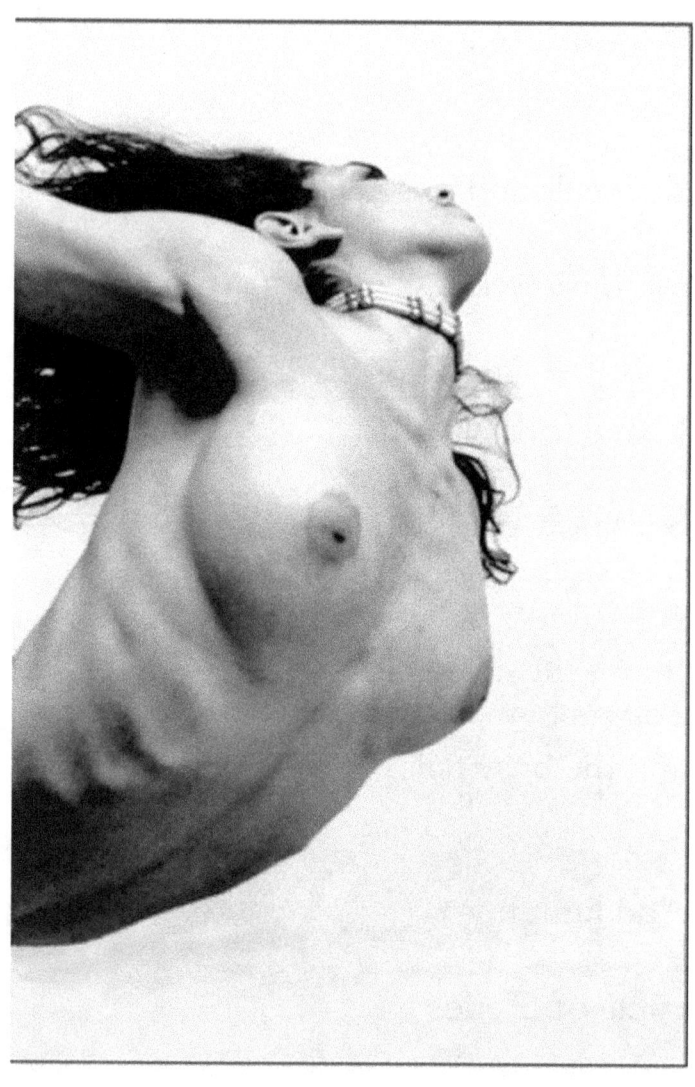

Lovers change

Once again somebody loves me

Once again somebody cares

Once again somebody's lover

Ain't no need for another

Memories are fading

of the last love I had

No more empty evenings

of the waiting

I had

to find a lover

ain't no need for another

and I'm getting over the last

Once again somebody loves me

Can't you tell somebody cares?

Once again my heart is aching

and I'm not fully aware

But the feeling is growing

and my face it is showing

Glowing and knowing

there's a love nest waiting for me

Once again, once again

I'm in love.

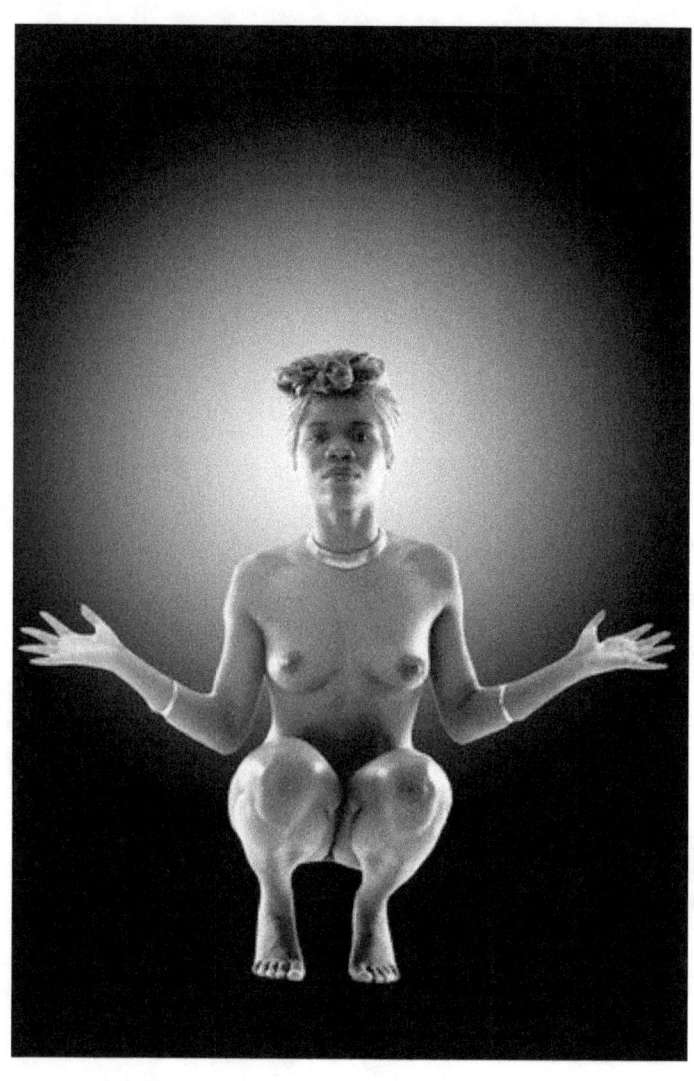

Sometimes

Sometimes

I can't wait

for night time to pass…..

The length of time

and increased crimes

of night time

Come on Sun…

        RISE !

sometimes

*I can't wait
for night time to pass...*

*The length of time
The increased crime
Of night time*

Come on sun...

RISE !

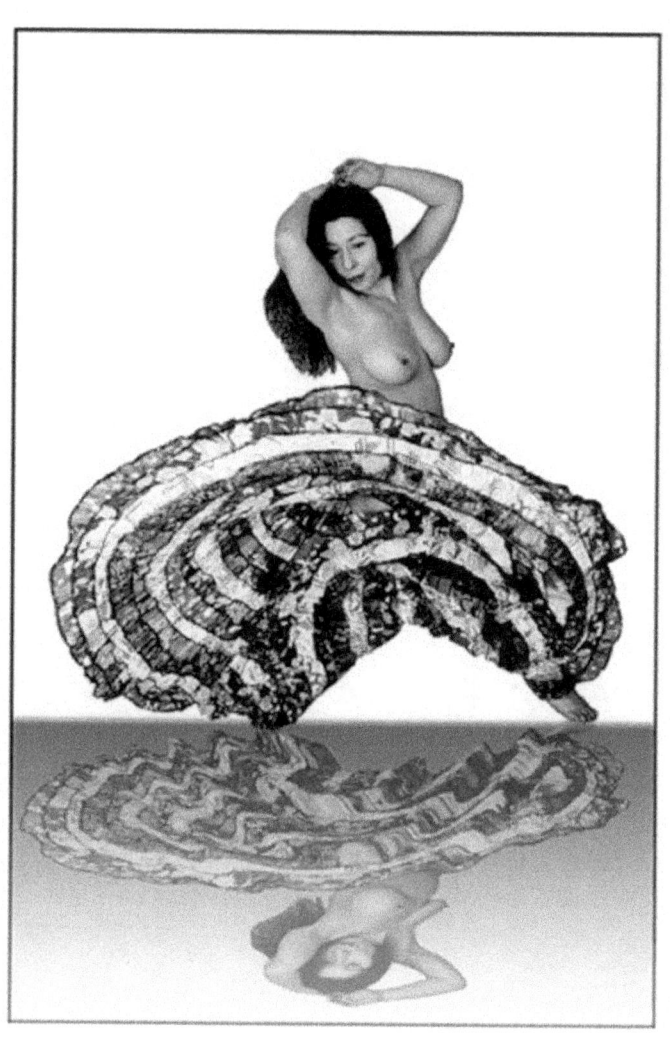

Hollywood Gold

Sipping Galliano to

the Hollywood Gold

I've donned my best chiffon this

night to match the star I hold

Endless beads are dripping from

the stage lights to the floor

Make-up streaking down my face as

the music starts to soar

I see a captive audience

blinded to the core

Clearly they have had enough

and still they yell for more

I've written many images on

that stage so full of song

Expended many energies on

nights sometimes too long

But I've lived one of the wonders

a girl dreams about

And sipped a taste of Hollywood

the Gold can't shine without.

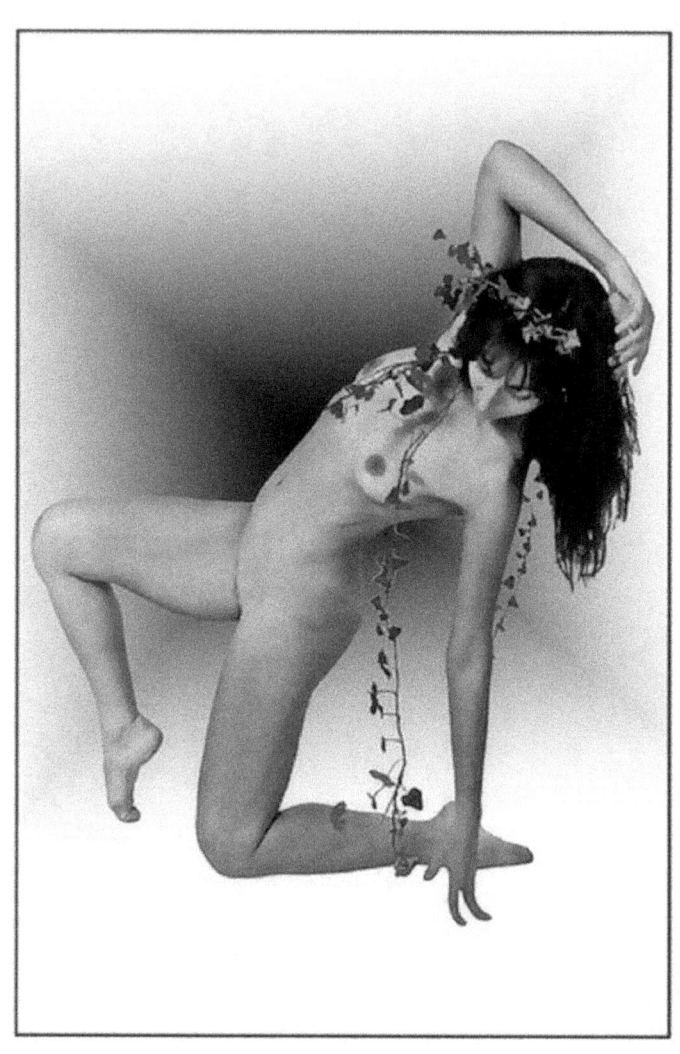

with a Latin flair

In that old Cantina

calamares on the grill

Thunder broke the silence and

the rain began to spill.

"Senorita" was voiced in

my general direction

The man lowered his head

as if ready for rejection.

Controlling his impatience

a loss was in his eyes

Desiring fulfillment

I'd fill before it died.

That man of quiet ecstasy has

taught me how to live

For in our English culture

we're never taught to give.

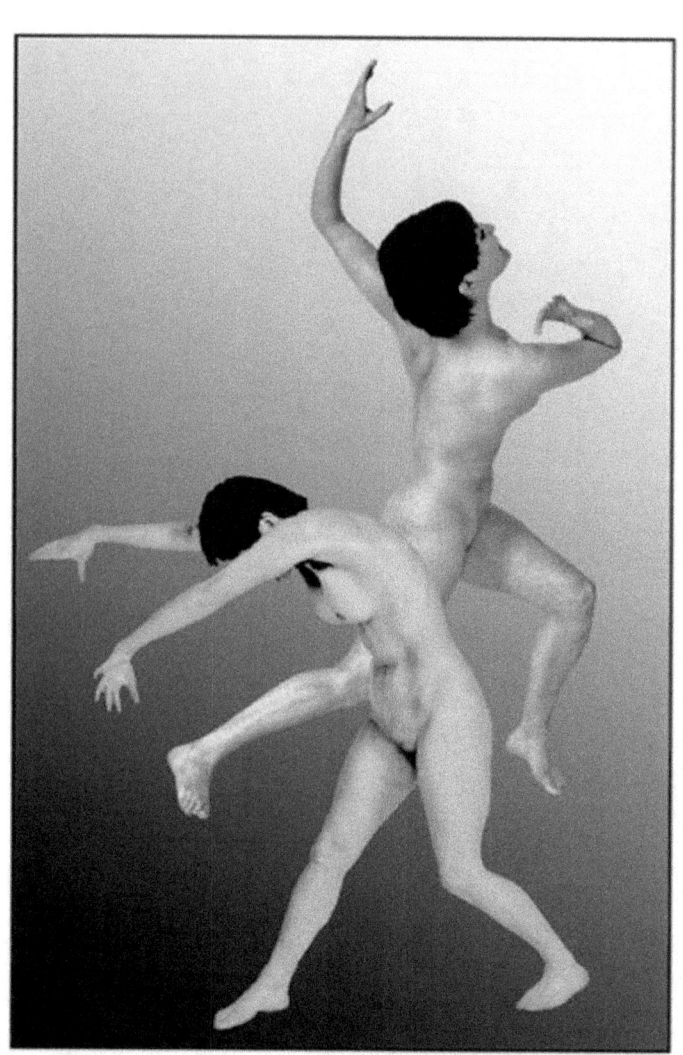

equal reality

For my beauty

I look up

to the skies

For my mind

I equal

my eyes

For my grief

I look

to the floor

But for my love

I look no more.

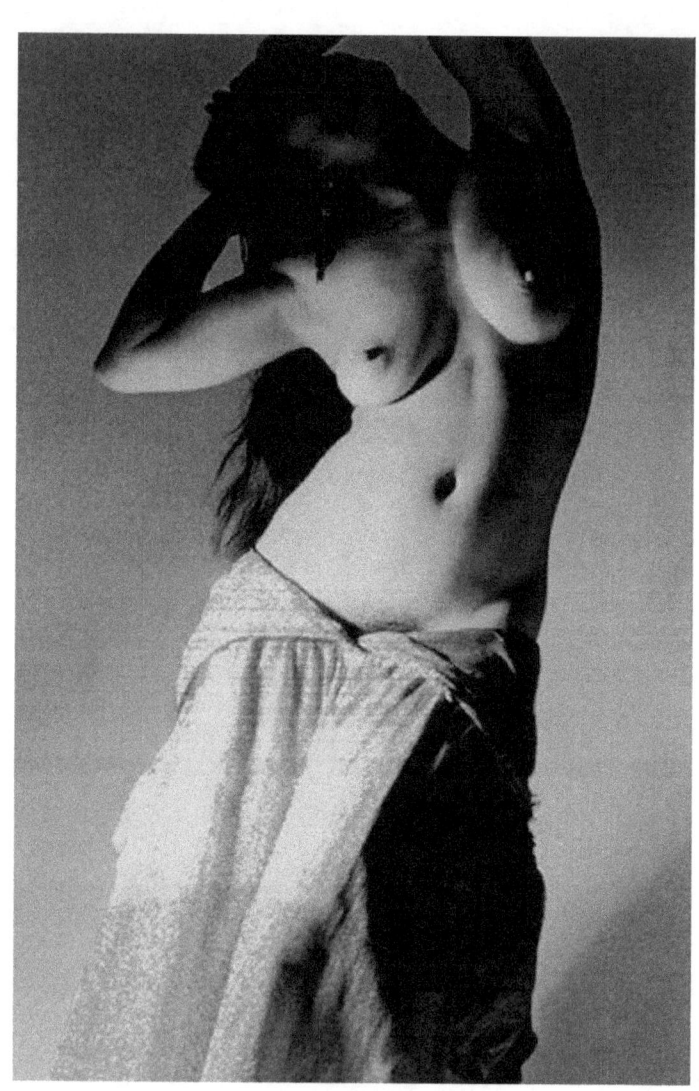

I find myself

With more refinement I'll go back

Back to the spontaneity

and energy I had

With more dedication and appreciation

of what I had

I'll go back

With the same sweet loving audience

and the same sweet affairs

I'll go back

I have the want

the need

and certainly the greed

But it's all I have left

that and the time to dream

of what I had.

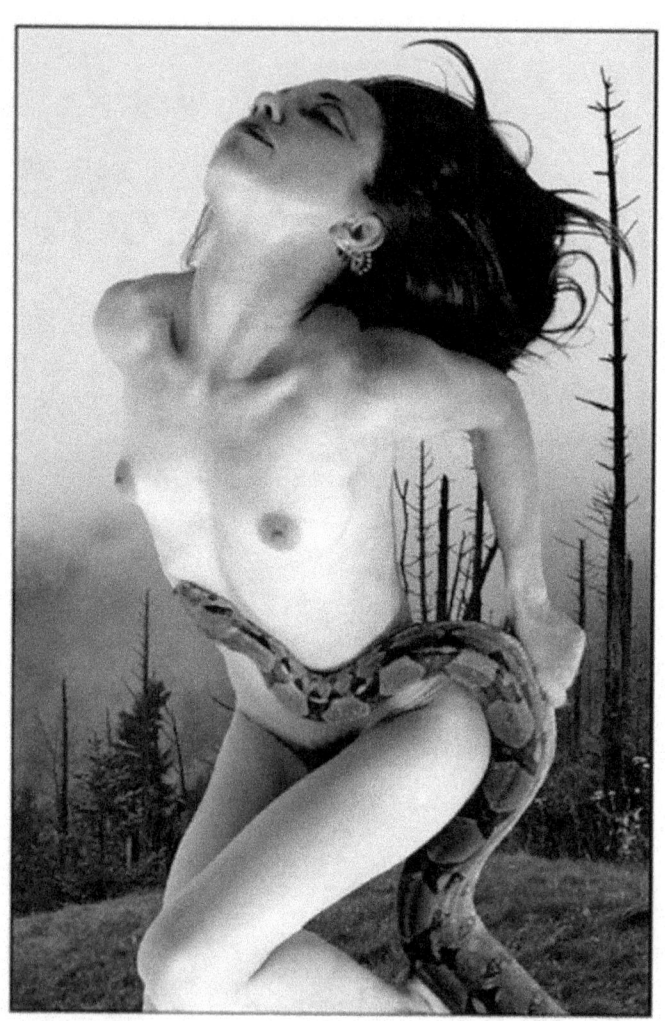

trembling

I feel a jungle trembling

I'm daring myself to hold you

to let my love go

to let the passion grow

But I'm needing your presence

as the days face the future

I want a child

through a man

who can make me

surrender like one.

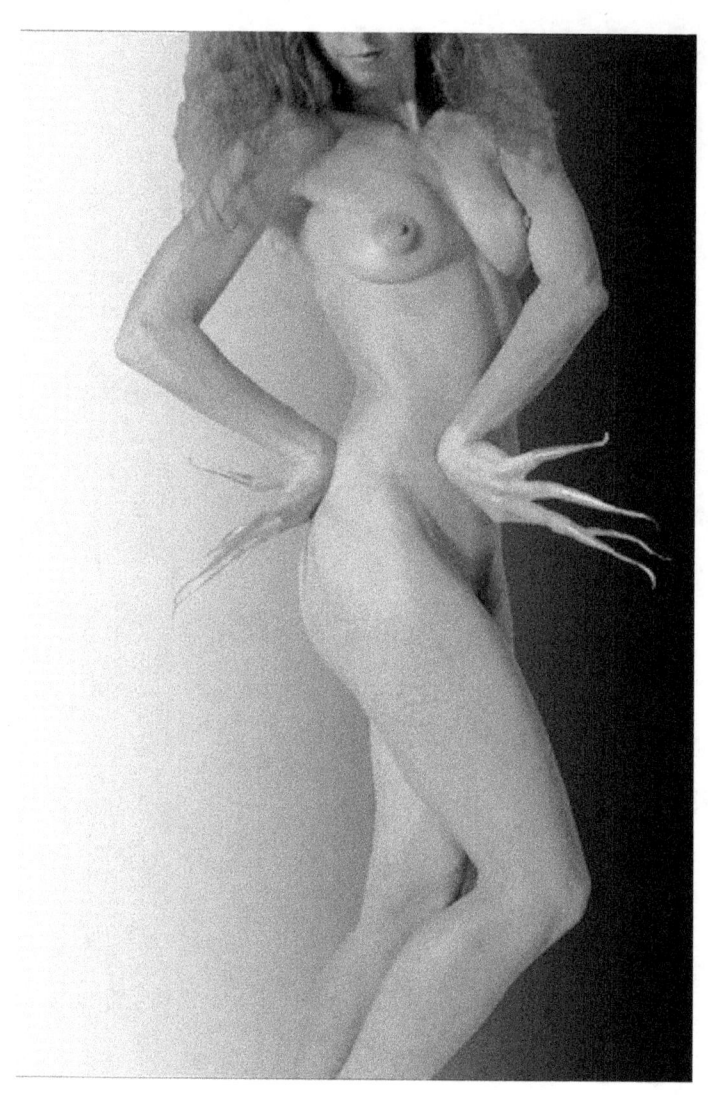

of sweet caring

Where does the sweet caring end

and the jealous worrying begin?

My love will be merely added prey

to my thoughtful caring

And will be a victim

of my thoughtless loss of love.

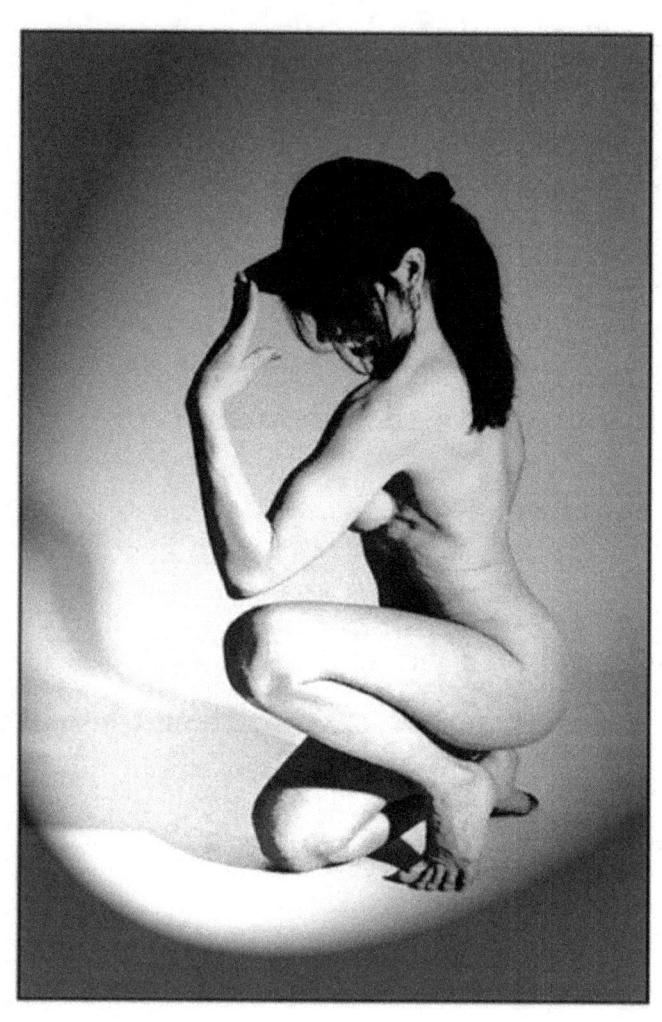

while kisses end

I wish a kiss

could blossom out

to last a lifetime

Instead

the feeling of ecstasy

is too short

Just like

my love for you

will soon come to an end.

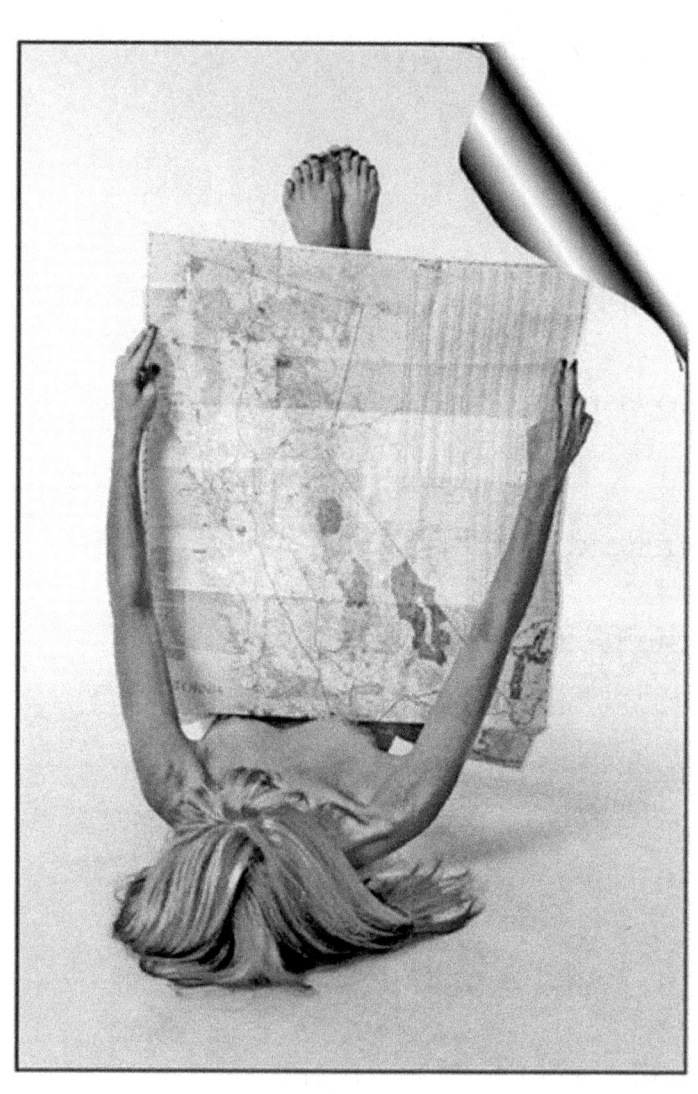

From California

What will it take

to make this diamond shine?

One year was not enough

to express what I needed

to make you feel.

I followed my scholastic destiny

then lost you while I slept

never knowing…

I keep this diamond with its fading glow

It seems to match my heart

and the love I'll never know.

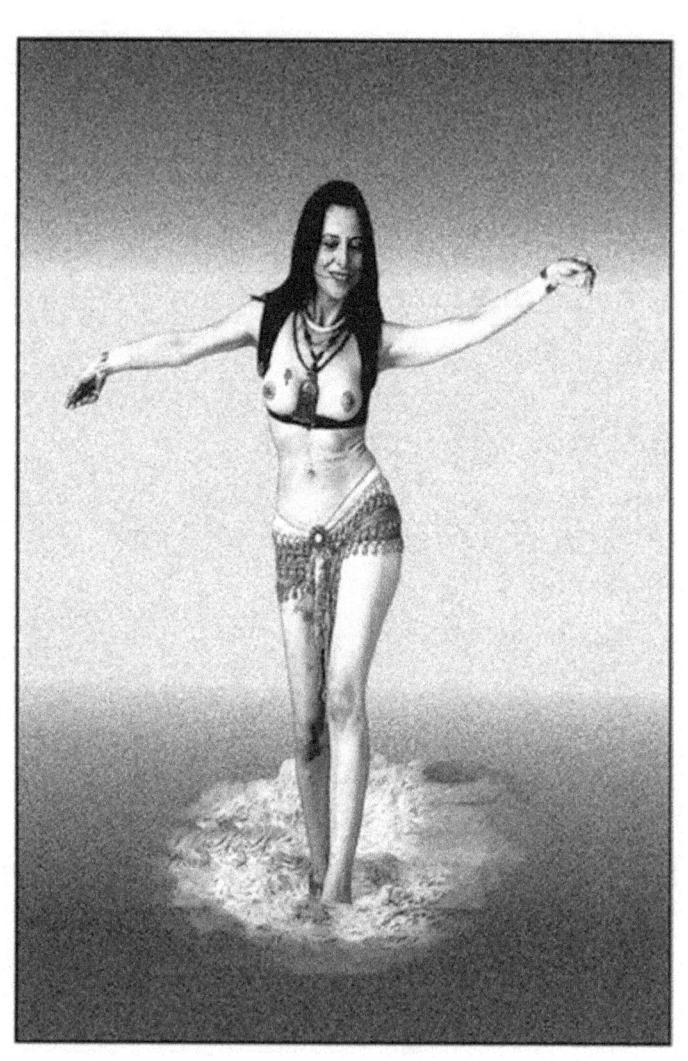

to Colorado

I left a lover I loved the most

I left a town I loved the best

I left some friends I respected more

than others I'd met in this town

But here lies a former part of me

I've decided I want back.

Here lies a professor whom I see

as a man a part of me.

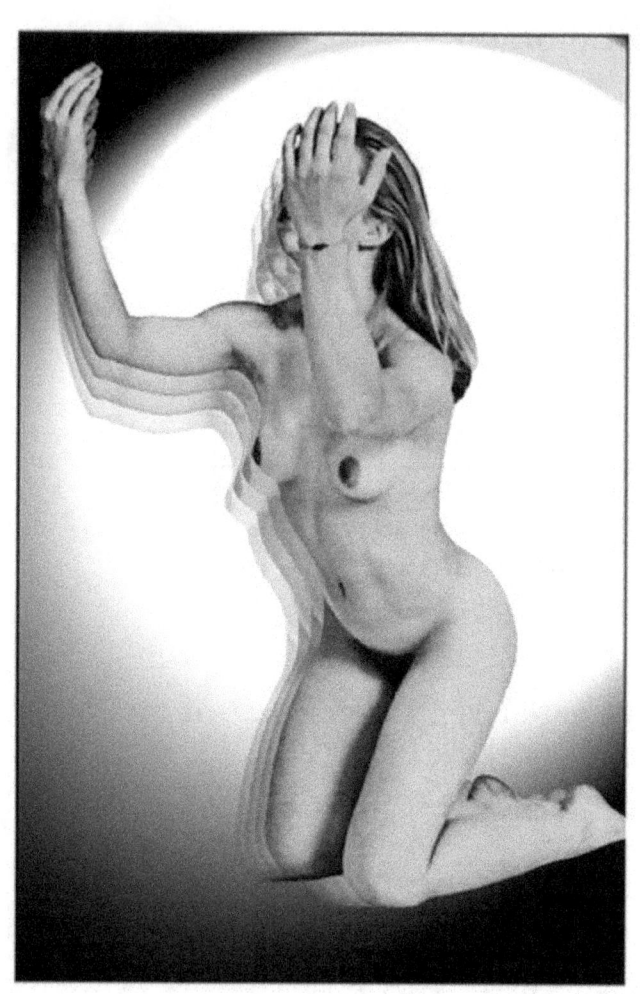

Always wishing

I wish the keys on my typewriter

were beating as fast

as the rain outside is feeding

each blade of grass

I wish the men I have known

could be molded into one

With their weaknesses omitted

my searching would be done.

I wish the scars were all healed

never leaving a trace

of the cracks on my heart

and those I saw break.

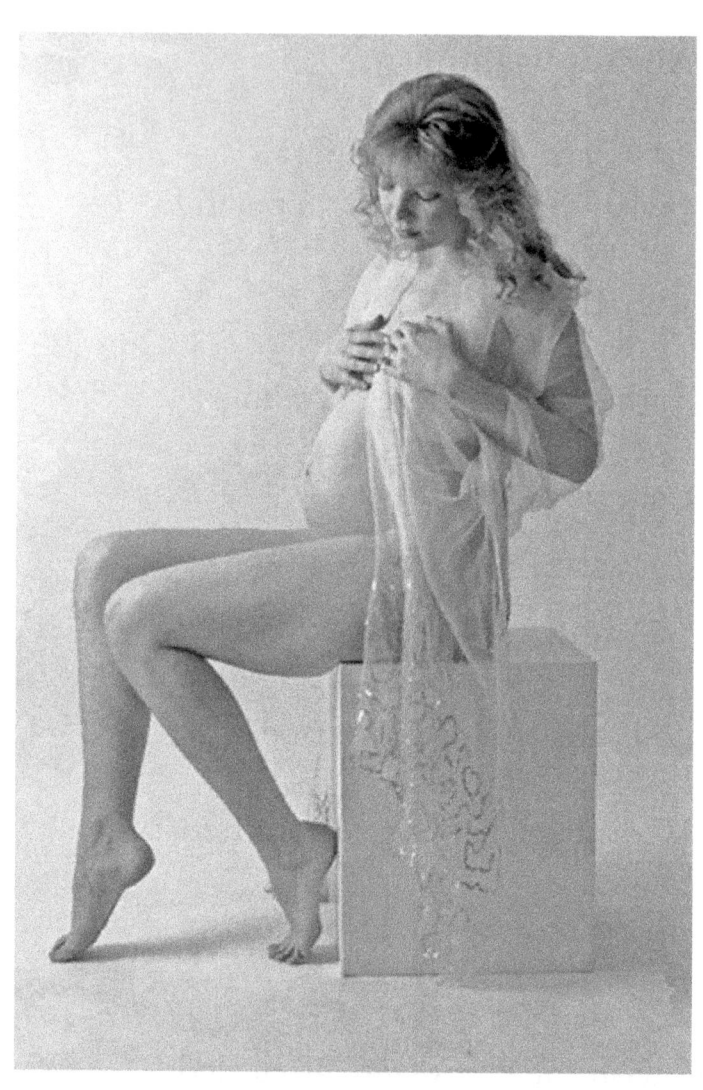

I was there

Through the friendships of many

came the eyes I would know

while the passion would wander

with sweetness and woe.

Through many years of searching

for the bliss I would find

was the spirit of wonder

in my new baby's eyes.

About the Authors

I have been writing most of my life – from short stories lyrics to columns - but I found poetry among the most satisfying.

The first poem I ever showed anyone was my 9th grade English teacher in Boulder, CO. I was nearly flunking the class due to my inability and refusal to study and comprehend grammar in the technical sense. I always liked writing but never felt the need to dissect it.

Finally we were given an assignment to write a poem for extra credit. Nearly everyone in class grumbled and struggled to rhyme something with "love" or "smiles," but I couldn't wait to do something I felt I could do well. The day after I handed in my poem, my teacher asked to see me after class.

To my shock, he accused me of copying it from a book. He said that a 14-yr-old was not capable of this level of thought. It remains one of the most memorable compliments I've had. Since he couldn't prove I didn't write it, he gave me a C.

Lesson Learned ~

Never let anyone discourage your art or judge your ability. Believe in yourself!

Bev Pogreba

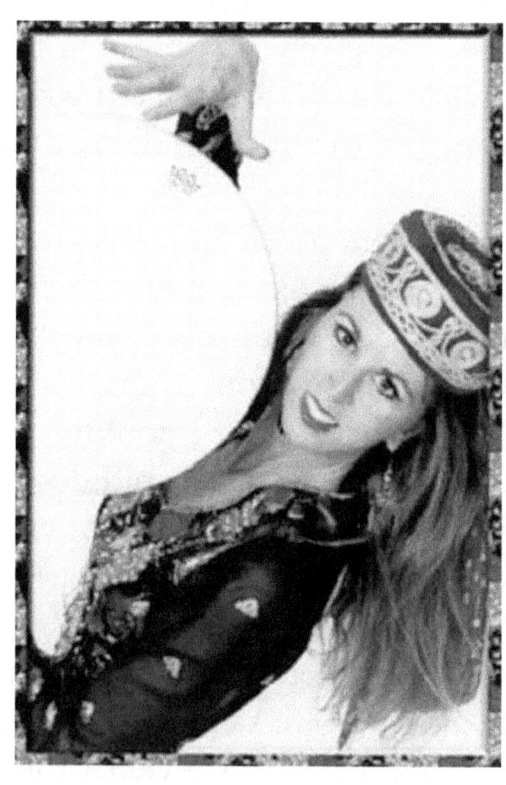

The images I have presented in this book are meant to reflect the mood and message of the poems.

A career embracing science, engineering and photography has contributed a unique blend of talents and knowledge to create this book combining poetry and photography. As a scientist, in industry and academia, I have invented, published papers and reports, established laboratories, received awards and attained international recognition. Engineering prepared me as a scientist to be disciplined and exacting through analysis and design.
My approach to photography has been influenced by these demanding careers as I strive to create worthwhile images. Using composition, design, discovery and being inquisitive has shaped a unique vision with original characteristics.

For a number of years I taught photography. My teaching approach made students aware of what and how they see as well as to use photographic tools and techniques too enhance and display their talents.

Several of the images in this book have been on display in art galleries. I have been in juried shows, been invited to show in galleries and have received a number of awards. Many of my pictures have been purchased for private collections.

Fritz Penning

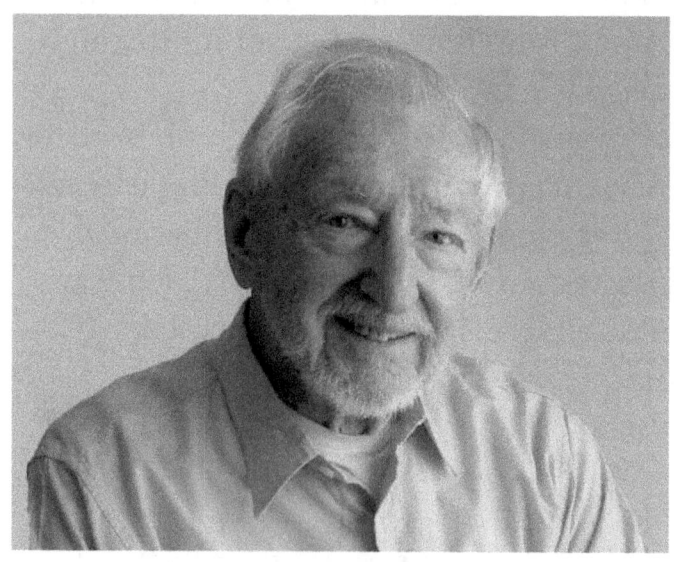

little girls

Little Girls
 trying hard to
 grow up fast.

But after reaching womanhood
 start
 searching for the past.

Their eyes
 have been overcome by
 lovers
 who would
 seize them.

They waited
 too long for
 the right man to
 please them.

growing up

It is my splendor
to have
them surrender
the imperfections
I dare to own.

I'd love to use them
abuse them
caress and then
mold them
to perfection.

trembling

*I feel a jungle trembling
I'm daring myself to hold you
   To let my love go
      To let the passion grow

But I'm needing your presence
As the days face the future

I want a child
Through a man
Who can make me
Surrender like one.

while kisses end

I wish a kiss

    *could blossom out
to last a lifetime.*

Instead

    *the feeling of ecstasy
is too short.*

Just like

    *my love for you
will soon come to an end.*

friends change

Cocktails and busytails
too busy to live

I have forty dreams
but know my limits

I limit the cocktails
and the busytails

And limit my
circle of friends.

lovers change

Once again
Somebody loves me
Once again
Somebody cares

Once again
Somebody's lover
And I'm not
fully aware

But the feeling is growing
and my face it is showing
Glowing and knowing
there's a love nest
Waiting for me

in love

You are
 the wings of
my dreams
 the pulse of
my spirit
 the root of
my soul.

The restless sea and
the endless sky
resemble the
crystal clear love
I will always express.

the dangers

Never will I be changed
into
another's image.

A fever
is beginning
to emerge.

Now all I need
is time energy and
space to breathe!

of sweet caring

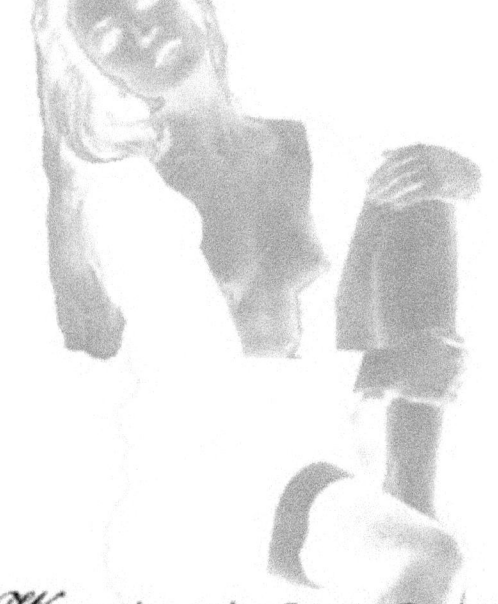

Where does the Sweet Caring end
And the jealous worrying begin?

My love will be merely added prey
To my thoughtful caring

And will be a victim
Of my thoughtless loss of love.

always wishing

I wish
the keys on my typewriter
were beating as fast
As the rain outside is feeding
each blade of grass.

I wish the men I have known
could be molded into one
With their weaknesses omitted
my searching would be done.

I wish the scars were all healed
never leaving a trace
Of the cracks on my heart
and those I saw break.

one day soon

With a love
I could have won
Came a love
I should have lost.

The pleasure of caring
loses its meaning
When the one you care for
decides
not to care.

How can you have
such a big heart
And break one
as big as mine?

Beauty is Forever

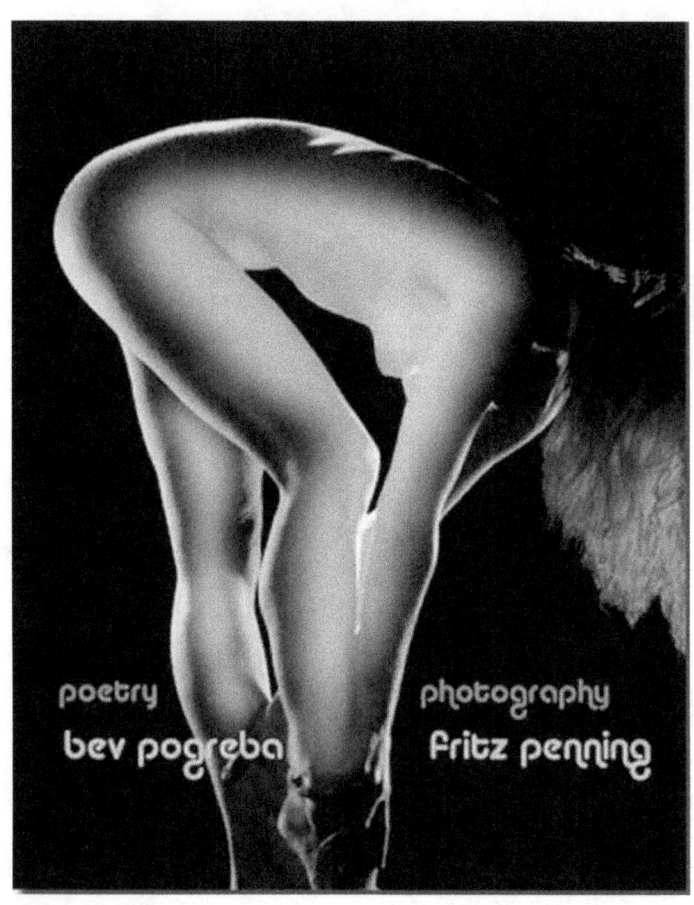

poetry
bev pogreba

photography
fritz penning

Other creations by Bev Pogreba ~

American Dancer – a Belly Dancing Story ~ *Based on a true story, a dancer immerses herself in Middle Eastern music and nightclubs in 1980s Hollywood. Humor, dating & culture ~ with a Twist!*

Chart Your Health 30 Day Journal *Track fitness, diet, stress, allergies, moods and more to help discover patterns in health issues. .*

Female Life in Poetry (Bilingual) *Poetry from "A Woman's Journey" in Spanish & English without photos.*

SEO Organics Easy Text Book *Search Engine Optimization and SEM made easy in white hat optimizing.*

Middle Eastern Belly Dance DVD *Cabaret and Folkloric dances of North Africa, Mediterranean, Central Asia, the Gulf and India.*